It doesn't mean anything when thicker over your head. At any r wind can blow and carry them away in an unknown direction.

You don't have to harm yourself if the world becomes difficult.

"I have to go through this again," said the cat as he watched Alice swallow several anti-depressant pills.

"Why would you do that, Alice? Has the world been cruel to you today?" the cat asked concernedly.

"Leave me alone," replied Alice, taking a sip of her tequila, which she drank on top of her medication.

"Don't be so rude. If anything happens to you, you won't have anyone to call for help," the cat warned, lighting a cigarette and squinting his yellow eyes.

"I know you're not going anywhere," Alice said. "You belong to me and I belong to you. Just let me survive this crisis." Well... Alice, the cat tugged on the tab. I understand what you're going through right now and I'm here for you. I just don't know what to say. Let's go see The Moon and The Eagle Owl.

"When the cat and Alice approached the horizon, they saw the Moon whispering to the Eagle Owl. As soon as they noticed the girl and the cat heading towards them, they stopped.

"Hello," said the Moon, attempting to smile and appear unbothered.

"How are you?" asked the Owl, pretending to inspect his claws.

The cat knew something was wrong but tried to remain calm for Alice's sake. "Hello, Moon. Hello, Owl," he said, squinting his left eye. We came to visit you, and I personally want to chat about what is going on in the World.

- look at her- cat pushed Alice towards them and Moon and Owl gasped.

"She is drinking tequila as if it were water." together with her antidepressants and tranquillisers.

"Alice was quiet, but her facial expression still conveyed a strong sense of sarcasm." Moon took a cigarette from a cat and began smoking it with her yellow hands. We have no impact anymore on the environment around us. Some souls made their choice, and now we just have to wait to see who will take over Evil or Kindness.

"Is it really that serious that a cat gave Alice a glass of water?" Yes, the Eagle Owl, who was usually very quiet, joined the conversation.

Yes! Everything is very serious, very bad. The Earth is covered in blood, and no one can help it.

People are infected by an untreatable virus, causing widespread panic This is a time when everyone is responsible for themselves. It is a war between good and evil, love and hate..

****

   Suddenly, Alice started to pay attention to what Cat, Moon and Owl were talking about.

"So what?" she said. I have to sit still and do nothing. I have to wait until the Red Plague destroys everything that matters to me, and then it will come further down to earth. And then what?" I want to fight it, Alice continued her monologue.

"It's madness, girl," said Cat, and Moon and Owl nodded in agreement. "You won't be able to change anything," Moon sighed quietly. "Believe me, if I'm absolutely powerless here, no one can help. I've already placed those two brothers on my surface as a reminder to humans that fratricide is the most heinous sin in the universe. They look at me almost every night, yet nothing will change what's going on in their hearts." Do you think that fratricide is only physical harm? Owl decided to step into this discussion. Not at all! Listen me out, please.

God created our Earth in seven days, and his tool was The Word. And that Word was good. Now ... everything you see around you—seas, oceans, mountains, the Moon and Son, and even me—are created by Him and His Great Will.

Alice listened attentively as the Owl spoke. Even Cat threw away his cigarette and nervously pulled his whiskers. The Eagle Owl continued, "And then He gave the biggest gift to humanity—free Choice. He loved and trusted His creators, who were made in His image and likeness." Therefore, people weren't happy with what they got. They let Evil manage their lives.

Jealousy, hate, fear, doubt and anger are emotions that originate in the human brain. These emotions were meant to help humans protect themselves and their children. However, they have left little space for love, which is essential for a happy and fulfilled life. As a result, a dark and destructive force emerged, which attracted many dark angels to land on Earth. Despite this, the world maintained a relative balance between good and evil. Unfortunately, this balance has now been disrupted, and evil is spreading its influence across the globe. It seems that many people have lost their ability to distinguish between right and wrong, good and bad, and have become too focused on their materialistic needs. They have stopped reading books and are not interested in teaching their children to read either. Being kind and honest is no longer popular, and the lines between truth and lies have become blurred. People are drowning in the superficial knowledge that they gather from electronic devices, and this has opened the gates to evil. Unfortunately, people like you and me cannot do much to stop it because there is a real war between the forces of good and evil. Step back and pray. Live your life and be happy that you're not one of those whose brains are totally infected by Digital Propaganda.

God exists and He always will. Trust him and you will see who is the Winner.

The owl suddenly stopped talking, flapped his wings and flew away.

Moon got pale and quiet. Cat took out a queuing cigarette and Alice threw her tequila in the Blue ocean.

The End

A selfish story

Alice yelled out "Cat!" from the living room. Cat responded from the roof, where he sat in a comfortable chair, sipping tea with a small amount of French brandy, "What??!!". Alice called him to come down and talk to her, as she was feeling nostalgic. Cat, uninterested, put on his sunglasses and crossed his back paws. There was no argument between them; it was just their usual battle of who was more selfish. Cat even complained to a seagull that he had always thought it was him. It was just a typical spring day. - I was sure it was me, and Cat moved a little pack of chips towards the seagull, encouraging her to listen to him out. Generally, he didn't care if someone else was listening; he just wanted an audience.

"Cat took a sip of his tea and smiled. 'But everything changed when I met Alice. She's an incredibly sweet and cute girl, but no cat can compete with her when it comes to selfishness. For example, when I wake her up at 5am because I'm bored and hungry, she just throws me out of the bedroom and shuts the door in my face.' Or...

she always tells me that I'm the most beautiful creature she has ever seen, but I've heard her say the same thing to her rabbits." She doesn't care about the danger of going outside on her own. What if something happens to her, and who'll take care of me then?!!!

"She's snoring, but if I snore, too, I'll be pushed out of the bed straight away. And her husband... Cat lit his pipe. Every time I think that Alice and I are finally alone in that big, comfy bed, watching our favourite programs, he comes and takes his place over and puts that stupid football on. And she lets him! You know, she lets him. Seagull looked shocked."- Sometimes I suspect that she loves him more than me.

"Do you have any chips left?" asked Seagull.

"Nope, but I have some cheese and crackers. Fancy?" replied Cat.

"Mmmmmm" Seagull mumbled with a bit of Mature Cheddar and oat cracker in his mouth. He liked Alice and knew that Cat loved food and could always be found around it. Cat confirmed this and added that he was always there for Alice, no matter what she needed. Alice called out for Cat, but he was busy drinking tea and asked her to wait. Despite being helpful, Cat also demanded respect and understanding from Alice as an independent person. Suddenly, Cat's nose caught a whiff of something delicious - he thought it might be ribeye steak. Excited, he jumped out of his chair and called out to Alice, asking if she had been looking for him. In a couple of minutes, he was sitting at the kitchen table, eating steak with blue cheese sauce, watching his favourite show and thinking that life is good.

   Seagull was asleep in The Cat's chair. He was dreaming about being a cat.

   The End.

Just domestic stuff

Alice loves coming back home after a long day of work, shopping or traveling. Her home is a beautiful place to relax and spend time with her husband and family members when they visit.

One of the things that makes coming home so special for Alice is her beloved cat, Mister Cat. He always welcomes her with a smile and is overjoyed to see her again.

One day, Alice returned home to find Mister Cat sitting at the kitchen table with his legs crossed, wearing glasses and reading some materials she had received from her psychologist. As soon as he saw Alice, his face lit up with a big smile and his green eyes turned to gold.

"The house was filled with an incredible fragrance that made Alice feel even more at home. "Wow!" screamed the Cat, "you're back! How was Paris?"

"Hi, my dear little friend," Alice was thrilled to see the clever ginger cat again.

"Everything was just great! It was an amazing trip."

"Where's your husband then?" the Cat asked..

- He went to a shop because there was no food at home. Do you have some?

Yep, I still have about 14 pouches left in the cupboard, a half bottle of milk in the fridge, a few drops of whiskey, and Mister Cat winked at Girl.

- Oh.... Don't mention alcohol now, please!

Alice looked a bit suspicious, in Cat's opinion.

- Why not? Have you been drinking a lot in Paris? You're a naughty girl!!! - Cat was waiting for the answer.

- No, not at all. I haven't been able to. Alice sighed.

- Why not?!! Paris is the capital of the best champagne in the world

   Not to mention French wine ☐ and brandy ☐. Mmmmm... with some very old cheese and croissants... Cat suddenly got back to reality after Alice threw at him a few peanuts; she was eating while listening to Mister Cat's imaginary story about tasty food and wine.

Alice was feeling a bit confused and disoriented. She asked, "When did you do that?" The other person responded with some possible scenarios, like after Alice's fourth whiskey, after a jug of pim, or maybe after she finished her rock n roll dance on the table and started feeling hungry after drinking a lot of beer. - You were "good" yourself- snorted Cat.

And started counting his fat , fluffy little fingers:

- singing in karaoke despite the fact that you absolutely cannot sing, getting into drinking competitions with a big block, shouting loudly at the crowd, and crying at the end of the party because you lost your lipstick...

- And who was responsible for that? - Alice asked. Who asked me to go there with you because we almost don't go out and it's boring and you feel lonely?

And then ... who added some tequila to my glass of Jin tonic?

Anyway, Grinch wasn't happy about us coming home at 3 a.m., laughing and making loud noises.

So when I tried to get a bottle of wine in Paris to have a lovely picnic next to the Eiffel Tower, he stopped me and said that he wasn't my fluffy bastard friend. He hasn't any desire to be involved in any party but sees some sights and goes to sleep.

 - He is a right wet blanket- said Cat. I feel sorry for you.

- Thanks, Cat, but I'm alright! I finally have seen the Eiffel Tower! - Alice got excited and continued - you can't even imagine how beautiful it was to be there in Autumn when it's still warm but leaves become ginger like you are, love in the air, and everyone is so fashionable and beautiful! The Tower is changing its colours at night, and the river Seine seems to be very deep and mysterious, but she's also a mirror of the Tower, and they are very close together.

 When you're standing there, on a very old bridge, you can't begin to imagine what those two things have seen in their lives!

 Too many things are coming out of your mind!

And Alice started to count—Musketeers, Queen Margo, Cardinals, intrigues, love and hate, brilliance and poverty, the meanness of courtesans, their love and cruel fight for the right to be a favourite in a King's eyes because it wasn't enough to just maintain your beauty....

And those taverns.... French food and wines.

"I was imagining the Parisian slums described in books by famous French writers like Victor Hugo, Alexandre Dumas, Stendhal, and Honoré de Balzac. I was thinking about the romance between Napoleon and Josephine, and the colours black, red, purple, and gold. However, I couldn't smell the strong aroma of Chanel No. 5 in the Parisian air. Cat listened to Alice without interrupting, captivated by the romantic musings.

"Next time you have to take me with you to Paris," Alice said. "I want to smell Chanel, see the Eiffel Tower, and talk with musketeers and courtesans!"

"Don't be soft, Alice," I replied. "They all exist in different centuries."

"So how do you know about them?" Alice asked.

"I read a lot," I said. "You should too. Then any of your trips won't be meaningless. You have to take care of yourself."

"Right," Cat said. "I'll get there soon enough. I promise." Then he asked, "Have you bought me any tasty treats?"

"Yes, I have," I said. "Here are some macaroons, cheese, and... frog legs in a tin!"

"Phew!" Cat shouted, running away from the kitchen. Alice was laughing at him because she had got a great revenge on that fluffy intriguer , thanks God she read a lot about it

The End

"The internal conflict of the Cat."

Part 1:

The moon has been hidden behind big clouds for a few days. The sky has been painted red and the weather forecast doesn't look promising for warm weather for the next few months. People are struggling to get into the Christmas spirit without resorting to antidepressants, alcohol or other substances. Despite the fact that the global atmosphere is not getting any better, Christmas is coming and people feel the need to keep it together, at least for the sake of the children. The Earth is still struggling with crimes, ongoing wars and general chaos, which is perpetuated by those who hold the power to press the Red button. The Cat couldn't sleep, he couldn't sleep at all for at least a two years, without using some sleeping pills, but then he wouldn't wake up until the mid-afternoon and he doesn't bother about it anymore.

 "Sir Cat has been pondering heavily about his own life as well as the lives of other cats and creatures in the world. The Girl is always busy and Cat doesn't feel like talking. He has already had a conversation with his mate from a different country where war was a daily occurrence, and he has been carrying the burden of that knowledge ever since." Tonight he has decided to go to the Wise Owl ☐ and confess all his worries about in order to get some answers and maybe, if he lucky , get back his sleeping ability….

Cat caught a night transfer of an old witch who was flying on her broom just before the first roosters started crowing. In a few minutes, he landed in a Magical Forest. It was a deep night, but the forest was illuminated by little fairies. These fairies were responsible for keeping the Magical Forest bright for its inhabitants, who only come out at night and sleep during the day.

The inhabitants of the Magical Forest make all important decisions, things, and impacts at night. This is to ensure that no human can disturb the process of the Big Surviving Program, which is a major document for those who live in the Magical Forest, the Kingdom of the Moon, and the Sun

Devoted Magicians. The old Wise Owl – Bruno lived in a big tree house on top of an oak tree.

His house was heavily fortified with a fence connected to the Truth-Shocking Therapy and surrounded by a Souls Mirrored wall. No one could enter without special permission from the Forest authorities, otherwise they would be overwhelmed by the ugliness of their own nature.

The Cat was granted permission and given a temporary password to access the house. He approached the house and repeated the phrase "Tea is important" three times, causing the Big Brown Gates, shaped like a giant brain, to open.

"Hi, Mister!" exclaimed Bruno, who had been eagerly awaiting the Cat's arrival. "What's up? Are you okay, my darling?" he asked as he led the Cat into the house with his big brown wing –.

"No really," Cat murmured under his nose as he got inside. "Okay!" said the Owl. "Let's get some tea! And you can tell me what's bothering you, and I will try to help you with it." "Do you have any scones or crumpets?" asked Cat. "It was a long way, so I went hungry..." "Yes, I have scones, crumpets, and even little mouse-shaped biscuits," said Bruno as he put a kettle on. "Why do we always have tea every time I come to visit you?" Robin, the Cat asked.- Because The Tea is a very special drink . You do not drink it with everyone. Tea it's personal, it's something which will calm your mind and open your heart ☐ towards your spiritual self and towards your spiritual mate .

"It will help you feel more connected to your inner nature, and I will be able to understand your thoughts," explained the voice. "So complicated," muttered Robin the Cat under his breath. "Shall we proceed?" asked Bruno the Wise Owl as he nibbled on a mouse-shaped biscuit.

Part 2.

After a few minutes of silence and tea drinking, Wise Owl initiated the conversation.

"So, tell me Cat, what brings you here to see me?" asked the owl.

"I have too many thoughts in my head and I can't keep them to myself anymore," replied Robin the Cat, looking at Bruno the Owl with hope.

Not knowing where to start, The Owl sensed Robin's hesitation and suggested, "Let's ask the Moon to join us. She always has a calming effect on you."

"Okay," said Mister Cat, and they sent a little fairy to ask the Moon to join them.

"Hello, guys!" greeted the beautiful face of the Moon as she appeared in the window. "I've heard you need me for some important reason?"

"It's Cat," said The Wise Owl. "I think he's feeling a bit depressed and needs to find some answers."

"Ah, I see," said the Moon, snitching a chocolate biscuit from the table. "Well, I'm here to listen. Let's get started." She settled back into the comfy, sheep-shaped cloud.

The conversation that followed was lengthy and emotional. Some of the forest's inhabitants witnessed the Cat crying while The Owl attempted to comfort him by stroking his head. The Moon was up and down on its chair, suspiciously changing some colours from pale white to dark brown. Eventually, after a few hours of talking, they all left the Owl House. The Wood's creators could see them hugging and then calling the Old Witch to bring the Cat back home. The details of their discussion were kept secret from outsiders, but it was evident that a decision had been made and more was yet to come...

To be continue .

"Alice's experiencing an internal conflict."

I'm just angry; I'm constantly angry. I got this state a couple of decades ago, and this is still the case, said Alice.

I've tried everything: meditation, church, confessions, spa, forgiveness, spiritual development, reading books, music, and listening to different gurus!

And I'm still very angry and my purposes of living are very vague.

There was a kind of life when I was a kid and your parents taught you to be kind and honest. But once you grew up the world changed in a second. Kindness became a punishment, and honesty became a way you will be hated and announced as a mental person.

How come once you are an adult, you don't belong to yourself anymore?

Everything is so complicated! Everyone tells you that you have to be kind and forgiving so..... they can do whatever they want to you.

I'm lost, I'm totally lost.

I'm not expecting anything new from this world. Let's just hope that after we dying we will really get to see those people who loved us the most.

Because if it's not the case, that only means that our lives are pointless.

Just to be clear

"I have a thought, Cat. I believe that being loyal is a trait of weak individuals or those who have been impacted by unfair actions of others," said Alice, who was clearly agitated.

Mister Cat remained quiet, but his silence conveyed more than any words could express.

"I used to think that obvious acts of evil would be immediately stopped by those who witness it. However, sometimes people are not immediately aware of bad things happening, and so they can't have an impact on it. But, if something is so obvious that you can touch it, see it, and hear it, then why would anyone play the game of 'loyalty'?" Alice lit a cigarette and continued, "What is the point? Someone's blood is thicker than water? Or maybe someone's children aren't as important? Would you act in the same way if your own interests were at stake? I bet you wouldn't care about loyalty if your house was on fire, or if your horse was drowning along with your other pets."

Alice took a drag from her cigarette before continuing, "It's easy for someone to present themselves as a helpful person who believes in providing choices to everyone."

She then asked another question, "Aren't those who possess all the power, money, and privileges supposed to protect those who depend on them? Hasn't the Lord granted them everything so that they could be proper leaders for their countries? For their people? For all creatures who can't defend themselves or feed themselves? What are they doing instead? What are they up to?"

"I'll tell you what they're doing. They are too busy making more money, acquiring more land, deceiving everyone and everything, pretending that they will never die. They are also pretending that they sit too high and that the pr0blems of somebody "down" are just a joke. They think they can decide who is going to live and who is going to die. Of course, what is one life worth compared to the business they have to deal with?"

There are many terrible things happening in the world, yet they are often disguised as something beautiful or glorious. How must an honest person feel about their life? Someone who has worked tirelessly to leave a small inheritance for their children and grandchildren, or someone who has sacrificed their health to provide for their family? Those in power who send bombs to destroy lives don't seem to care about the human cost; they only care about achieving their goals. However, I believe that those who cause the tears of an old lady, a mother who has lost her son, or a child who is scared by an air attack, will ultimately pay the price for their actions. The biggest castle with all its luxurious furniture and art, built by thousands of skilled workers, is worth nothing in the eyes of God compared to a humble hut built by an honest person who has worked hard to provide a roof over their family's heads.

The end

About customer service

Alice overheard a conversation between Mister Cat and a selling assistant at a grocery store. Mister Cat had suggested to the assistant that using her brain would be beneficial, even though he wasn't a stylist. Alice asked him what had happened, to which he explained that the assistant had been rude to him, perhaps because she had never seen a cat shopping for himself. The assistant had made fun of Mister Cat's hat and bow tie and commented that it was strange to dress up for grocery shopping. She had also made a joke about her dog tearing Mister Cat's outfit apart if it was there. Alice was concerned about Mister Cat's well-being and asked if he was okay.- Yes , I'm absolutely fine now. I've told her that I'll complain to her management about this incident.

- Yes, you definitely have to do it- said Alice and opened a car door .

They were driving quietly. That kind of attitude has shocked both of them and they were trying to digest what had happened in the store.

And then it wasn't much to add.

Mister Cat filed a complaint with a customer service team and was told that the situation would be resolved immediately. The seller assistant responsible for the issue was fired. However, the real problem wasn't about punishment, the victim, or the abuser. The true issue was the lack of humanity, tolerance, and understanding towards things, people, and creatures that are different from oneself. It's important to broaden our horizons, learn, love, and respect the differences that make our world so unique. Ignorance can cause serious harm, and it's crucial to be mindful of our actions and words to avoid causing harm to others.

The End

"Does the word 'lonely' have a negative connotation, as if it implies wickedness?"

"You know Alice, Cat was looking at the moon and smoking his pipe," said the speaker.

"You know that some people are very bad at being lonely?" Alice responded, smiling at the speaker. "You probably remember," she continued, "how many times we were stalked with you."

"By the way, Cat," Alice asked, "do you think that stalking has anything to do with socializing?"

"I don't think it does," replied Cat, pouring himself a glass of milk. "Personally, I think that stalking is the last stage of loneliness and is already an illness."

"Agreed," Alice said. "But why would someone be that way?"

"Sometimes people exhibit certain behaviors due to various triggers," Cat said thoughtfully. "For instance, some individuals were abandoned by their parents, while others were rejected by their partners and found it hard to move on. And some people simply believe that their behavior is normal." Alice was washing dishes and planning her reading for the evening. She knew the type of person Cat was referring to - the ones who struggle to be alone with their thoughts and need someone else to validate their self-worth. Too many things have been said and done in their past, which makes them seek companionship as a form of reassurance..

If you recall our first trip to the Moon, Cat blew a kiss to the big white face that appeared in the window. If you do remember, you might also remember those shadows fleeing from the light. People are often scared of confronting their true nature and are content to walk in darkness, occasionally preying on others by making them feel sorry for themselves. But the real problem is that many people believe they need someone else to make them happy or at least feel better. - And if it's not happening? - asked Alice

"I will remember the following text for you:

"They became aggressive, self-damaging, and turned to false religions or theories. They hated everyone around them and believed that someone else controlled their lives.

"Isn't it ridiculous?" The girl sighed.

Cat brought up the topic of stalking and mentioned that if someone is nice to another person, that person may try to manipulate them into being responsible for everything they are going through. It's important to protect oneself and not waste time and energy on things they don't want to be involved in. Alice was a bit confused and asked if she shouldn't help someone who is lonely and complaining about their life, who will?- Alice, Cat stroked her head and said- you're not A God , you're girl you can't take responsibility about another human being choices. You can just take a proper care of yourself and me ... because I'm your pet and I can't look after myself properly.

"All those stalkers need to realize that they have a problem and learn how to deal with it. What did you do when you weren't happy with yourself?" asked Cat.

"I was developing myself," replied Alice. "I read a lot, worked hard, went to the gym, watched educational movies, talked to psychologists, and tried to make myself better and smarter. I also reflected on my mistakes and tried to correct them. Of course, I had a lot of dark moments, but I didn't blame anyone else for them."

"You see," said Cat happily, "if you are unhappy, work on yourself, make yourself better, and the world will become a better place for you."

"Of course," Cat's voice went quiet, "we have to mention that you don't have to do it alone. There are many services out there to help you."

"By becoming a better version of yourself, you'll see how ridiculous your feelings were before," Cat concluded.

The End

Statement of the Cat

Cat stood in the middle of the room and cleared his throat. All of his friends were present, waiting for him to speak. The only one not present in the room was the Moon, who was watching from the sky wearing headphones connected to a computer that was filming the event.

Cat started his monologue, "Dear friends and family, dear mates and enemies! I feel like I have to say this right here and right now. I want to thank everyone here today. Thank you to those who have turned their backs on me, because of you, I learned to rely on myself and my God only. Thank you to those who have betrayed me, because of you, I learned to be more careful with some people." Thank you those , who stole from me, because of you I learned that all material things can be replaced but trust is very fragile.

Thank you those , who left me. Because of this I met those people, who really worth to be in my life and appreciate more those, who never leave.

"I would like to express my gratitude to those who have taken opportunities away from me, as it has helped me find better ways to develop myself. I am also thankful to those who have envied me, as it has taught me to appreciate my work more. Your envy proves that I am doing something special. To those who have hated me, thank you for confirming that I have the strength to move forward with dignity and respect. To those who have laughed at me, I am grateful for the challenge as it has made me stronger. Thank you to those who have hurt me, as it has shown me that I have the ability to recover. Lastly, thank you to those who have triggered my bad side, as it has allowed me to see it and work towards becoming a better person."

And thank you to those who have always been there for me, who have loved and supported me always. You know that our relationship has always been equal ☐. Thank you so much for standing by me during some rainy days; it was hard, it is hard, but our sunny days are so good ☐. And, finally, I want to say thank you to myself for being patient with all of you and always looking for ways to forgive and forget. It's not my fault that I'm better than anyone else... Friends started laughing. "It won't be the cat," said Alice. "He really thinks that," the moon was laughing too. "I know," said the owl ☐. The cat looked satisfied, and he was about to join his mates, the seagulls, and have some food.

The End

About previous life

"I once wore many beautiful dresses made of silk, guipure, brooch, and adorned with a huge amount of lace. I also wore batiste collars and cuffs. These garments smelled so pleasant, with a fresh new fabric scent from far-off lands, seas, and mountains. I even had a veil or a hat on my head, and beautiful girls with long blonde hair dressed me up, making me feel like a queen," Alice shared with excitement.

The Cat asked curiously, "With what did the clothes smell so good?"

There was a lot of velvet, gilding and mahogany carved wood around. White and red roses grew in the cherry orchard behind a white vintage window. And there lived a great white parrot...

There were black peonies in a vase on the table.

And the bitter scent of some perfume around and dark blue clothes in people ....

And next to the vase, on the table, is a glass of burgundy and blue grapes.

- That was before our meeting? - The cat looked closely at the girl.

- I forgot...

I need to remember. I'm pretty sure this has happened to me.

I've been feeling disconnected from something very important my whole life.

I need to be somewhere else....!

And also.... she whispered... There was also a carriage and horses and on the horses there were huge, dark burgundy pompoms, carriage windows hung with dark blue lace...

What kind of mirage is living in my head? Where is this place ?

- Alice, don't worry, you'll definitely be back there! - The cat put a soft paw on her shoulder.

I belive you.

- But when?

- When you remember.

And you will definitely remember.

And believe me, it's unlikely they forgot about you there. I'm sure everyone is looking for you.

- But what happened....? - sadly asked Alice. And she herself started to answer:

- I think I was bewitched or punished by sending me to live in another time space.

- And now she walks through forests and swamps at night and howls. Looking for his prince, the Cat made a joke and got a slap right away.

- Prince... Cat... You are a genius but your evil.

You're right I think my prince is in another dimension.

"It is likely that he is also under the spell of the Wicked Witch. However, I have a feeling that he is nearby. It's as if we are both walking along different sides of the same great wall, unable to find a door. But we will definitely find her, and when we do, everything will fall into place," said Alice.

"Why is the Witch evil?" asked the Cat.

"Because she doesn't love anyone, and therefore nobody loves her. Without love, the soul dries up, and the heart becomes hard," replied Alice.

The Cat put its paws on its head in contemplation.

The End

No name needed

Come with me - Alice the Cat stealthily summoned.

They quickly jumped off the branch of the old one as the world of oak and quietly followed toward the horizon.

- We are walking on the moon's path across the sea. The cat grabbed Alice's hand, and she felt the cold glass under her feet. The sea slept, and the Cat, afraid to disturb its peace, walked on tiptoes.

Alice has followed his example.

When the Moon was already very near, the cat leaned on her and smoked his pipe.

- Alice, I want to show you what the moon sees while on the horizon.

People usually look at her across the sea or through the mountains or from the balconies of their houses, but no one ever wondered what she sees.

Luna finished talking to Filin and turned to them.

Moon, tell me, what do you see? - childishly asked Alice. Cause I don't see anything but your path and the flashes of the waves.

Alice... I only see what I shine. But I myself decide where to shine and what covers to lift.

And how do you know what you want to see? - The cat obviously knew the secret, but today it was a guide.

- I hear smells and follow them.

- How's that? - Alice felt like a child.

- Everything has its smell - continued the Moon. Let's go.

The cat and Alice grabbed her braids and they flowed smoothly along the horizon.

- How do you feel now, Alice? - The moon has stopped

- I can smell the smell of fresh roses, with hints of cardamom and cinnamon.

-This is what happiness smells like. The moon directed one ray in the direction of the spicy aroma and they saw a small crib in which a pink-cheeked baby was lying, and nearby, holding hands were his father and mother. They felt someone's presence and turned to the window with a smile.

Luna smiled back and gently threw a couple of golden freckles on the baby's nose.

- After a couple of miles, the moon repeated the question:

- How do you feel now, Alice?

- The smell of red pepper, notes of peony, the aroma of tart wine, vanilla and the fragrant aroma of pomegranate.

- That's what passion smells like and the Moon threw a beam, exposing a man and a woman, who, like a bonfire, danced their fiery Flamenco on the shore of the blue sea.

The company flew on. The Cat acted like an expert all this time. Apparently it was not his first night walk.

- And now, Alice, the Moon seemed serious.

- Phew... the girl covered her nose.

I smell bile, burning coal and something very sour. It's like vinegar but worse.

- What is this ???

- The moon smiled sadly. - This is how unfulfilled hopes, deceived souls, overworried happiness, and the fireplaces of the soul smell.

Brrrr... How scary! The Cat is eating. So, Moon, will you shine here, too?

- Of course, she also threw her big beam into the dark.

Neither Cat nor Alice saw anything but fleeing shadows.

- Where are they running to ???? - the girl was confused.

- they run away from themselves, afraid to see their ugliness in the moonlight.

Fools..... I give them light so they can find their way and smell different but they are afraid.... What they most fear is seeing their true, distorted by pain. And this fear is stronger than their desire to become happy.

The moon turned away quickly. Everything got quiet around, and in the dark, you could only hear Alice howling and the cracks in the cat's smoking pipe.

The End

Epilogue:

"You see, Cat, they want to control me," Alice thoughtfully said. "They don't understand that I am allowing them to do this so that I can see how far their government can go."

The Cat looked up at the sky, and the moon was reflected in its narrowed eyes. "Yeah," he said. "It's stupid. They don't even realize that they are trying to control a force that can engulf them like a tsunami at any moment."

To be continue …..

Printed in Great Britain
by Amazon